CW01151664

Original title:
Holly and Frost

Copyright © 2024 Swan Charm
All rights reserved.

Author: Liina Liblikas
ISBN HARDBACK: 978-9916-79-969-7
ISBN PAPERBACK: 978-9916-79-970-3
ISBN EBOOK: 978-9916-79-971-0

Evergreen Silhouettes Against the Snow

Tall pines stand proud and bold,
Casting shadows, secrets told.
Their green lives stark against the white,
Guarding whispers of the night.

Snowflakes dance on frozen eaves,
Nature's quilt, a tapestry weaves.
In silence, beauty's glory glows,
Evergreen silhouettes in rows.

A Tinge of Red in the Frosty Air

Crimson leaves still cling to trees,
Sending warmth in winter's breeze.
Berries bright, a vibrant show,
Against the chill, they fiercely glow.

In gardens bare, a splash of cheer,
Whispers of spring whisper near.
The cold can't steal such lively shades,
A tinge of red, where beauty wades.

Celebration of Life Beneath the Cold

Beneath the frost, the earth sleeps tight,
Yet life persists, a hidden light.
In winter's heart, dreams still ignite,
Petals wait for spring's delight.

Small creatures scurry, secret plans,
With hope that dwells in quiet spans.
A celebration in silence bold,
Life whispers sweet beneath the cold.

Seasons of Whimsy in Twilight's Glow

Dusk descends with playful grace,
Painting shadows on a familiar place.
Whimsy dances in the fading light,
Seasons blending, day and night.

Stars peek out, a twinkling cheer,
While moonbeams smile, drawing near.
In twilight's glow, magic is found,
Whispers of seasons spin around.

Shimmering Boughs at Dusk

In twilight's gentle glow we stand,
Shimmering leaves, a soft command.
Whispers dance in the cool night air,
Boughs sway lightly, a secret prayer.

Stars peek through the branches tight,
Casting dreams in fading light.
The world slows down, the heart takes flight,
In this magic, all feels right.

A Tale of Green and Grey

The forest breathes with life anew,
Emerald under skies of blue.
Yet shadows creep where silence lies,
A tale of green, where grey defies.

Mossy stones mark paths once tread,
Between the hues, the stories spread.
In every leaf, a whisper's thread,
Of nature's dance, both bright and dread.

Crimson Clusters in the Cold

Beneath the frost, red berries cling,
In winter's grip, their colors sing.
Crimson clusters, a feast for eyes,
A promise held under icy skies.

Nature's heart beats strong and bold,
As frigid winds brush off the cold.
Life persists, a tale retold,
In vibrant hues, the warmth we hold.

The Touch of Winter's Hand

With each soft flake that falls like dreams,
The world transforms into silver streams.
Winter's hand caresses the ground,
A quiet magic, so profound.

Bare branches draped in a cozy shawl,
Nature rests, heeding winter's call.
In stillness, hear the gentle thrall,
Of peace and beauty, embracing all.

Enchanted in the Frigid Light

Beneath the moon's soft glow,
A world of dreams takes flight.
Whispers of the night breeze,
Enchanted in the frigid light.

Snowflakes dance in silence,
Covering all in white.
Magic lingers gently,
In the heart of winter's night.

Trees adorned with crystals,
Sparkle in the starry sight.
Lost in winter's wonder,
Enchanted in the frigid light.

Carpets of Ice and Petals

Beneath our feet, a treasure,
Carpet of ice so bright.
Petals frozen in stasis,
Caught in winter's bite.

Each step a soft whisper,
Nature's breath, pure delight.
A world transformed and glistening,
Carpets of ice and petals unite.

Colors blend with the frost,
In a scene that's pure dynamite.
Nature's art displayed so well,
Carpets of ice and petals in sight.

A Time of Twinkling Stars

In a vast and silent sky,
Stars begin to twinkle bright.
Whispers of a timeless song,
A time of twinkling stars ignites.

Dreams unfold like petals,
Bathing in the cosmic light.
Guided by the distant glow,
A time of twinkling stars in flight.

Each twinkle tells a story,
Of love, of hope, of plight.
We stand beneath their canopy,
A time of twinkling stars, our sight.

Secrets of the Snowed-in Forest

In the hush of winter's cradle,
Secrets lie deep in white.
Underneath the blanket cold,
A story hidden from the light.

Whispers of the trees above,
Tell tales of day and night.
Footprints vanish with each breath,
Secrets of the snowed-in forest's might.

Creatures take their refuge,
Feeling safe and out of sight.
Nature holds its wonders tight,
Secrets of the snowed-in forest ignite.

A Symphony of Color in White

In winter's grace, the world is bright,
A dance of colors, pure delight.
The sunlit shades on snowflakes play,
In this serene, enchanted sway.

Crimson berries, branches bare,
Golden leaves float through the air.
Each hue a note, a vibrant sound,
A symphony where peace is found.

Sapphire skies in twilight gleam,
With silver whispers, soft as dreams.
The palette shifts, a fleeting show,
Where nature's art begins to glow.

The Spirit of Amber and Chill

In autumn's breath, the colors change,
Amber glow and shadows strange.
Chill winds beckon, crisp and clear,
While golden leaves begin to cheer.

A setting sun, a warming hue,
Beneath the trees, a world anew.
The spirit stirs in twilight's grace,
As amber whispers fill the space.

Fires crackle, shadows dance,
Nature's lullaby, a soft romance.
In every heartbeat, change is still,
The essence held in amber chill.

Dreams of Green in the Frost

Beneath the frost, the earth sleeps tight,
In dreams of green, the hearts ignite.
Silent wishes weave through the chill,
Hope unfurls, a tender thrill.

Emerald whispers in the night,
The scent of earth, a pure delight.
Nature knows of spring's embrace,
In winter's heart, the dreams still race.

Each frosted blade, a story spun,
Of life that waits for warmth and sun.
In hush of snow, beneath the frost,
The dreams of green are never lost.

Whispers Beneath the Snowflakes

Whispers rise with falling snow,
Silent secrets, soft and slow.
Each flake a tale, a fleeting breath,
In winter's quiet, life and death.

Underneath the blanket white,
Roots dig deep in soft twilight.
Nature rests, but dreams arise,
With every flake that graces skies.

Patience wrapped in whispers light,
In the silence of the night.
Beneath the snow, the earth will sigh,
Awaiting warmth, a gentle cry.

A Glimmer in the Gloom

In shadows deep, a light appears,
A whisper soft that calms our fears.
It dances gently, hope's embrace,
A fleeting moment, time and space.

Against the dark, it stands so bold,
A story of the brave retold.
Through trials faced, it lights the way,
A promise blooms at break of day.

From ashes gray, the fire grows,
In every heart, a spark bestows.
With every step, we rise anew,
A glimmer bright, forever true.

Crimson Leaves and Silver Dreams

In autumn's heart, the leaves ignite,
A symphony of red and light.
Each rustling whisper wears a sigh,
As dreams take flight beneath the sky.

The silver moon plays hide and seek,
While shadows dance, the moments peak.
A fleeting glance, a tender gaze,
In golden hues, the world displays.

Through tangled woods, where silence dwells,
The stories born, the magic swells.
In every breath, a secret seams,
We wander lost in silver dreams.

The Silent Shroud

A blanket thick, the fog descends,
In whispered tones, the silence spends.
The world recedes, a soft embrace,
We drift in quiet, timeless space.

Through shadowed paths, we gently tread,
Where echoes linger, whispers spread.
In muted hues, the night's parade,
A canvas rich, where thoughts cascade.

The stars hold watch, in solemn grace,
While dreams weave tales we dare not trace.
In tranquil depths, we find the sound,
A symphony from silence found.

Winter's Lament

The world is wrapped in icy breath,
As nature weeps a frosty death.
Each flake a tear, a silent plea,
In winter's heart, all warmth will flee.

The trees stand bare, their branches cry,
Beneath the weight of leaden sky.
Yet deep inside, a spark remains,
A hope that fights through chilling pains.

In every storm, the spirit braves,
Though cold may haunt, the heart it saves.
For spring will come, with colors bright,
To banish shadows, reignite light.

Glistening Jewels on the Earth's Blanket

Morning dew glistens bright,
Like jewels on emerald green.
Nature's treasure in soft light,
A tranquil, serene scene.

Petals glimmer, colors burst,
Each one a story, a sigh.
In the meadow, joy is first,
As whispers of spring fly.

Gentle breeze brushes by,
Caressing leaves in delight.
Underneath the vast, blue sky,
The landscape gleams in bright light.

Rainfall weaves a silken sheet,
Covering earth with a hymn.
Streams of silver at our feet,
A world wrapped in nature's whim.

In shadows where silence dwells,
Glistening secrets softly glow.
Nature's beauty always swells,
In moments, pure joy flows.

The Dance of Nature's Jewel Tones

Emerald leaves sway and shine,
In the rhythm of the breeze.
Crimson blooms in perfect line,
Nature's dance that aims to please.

Amber sunlight filters through,
Casting gold on dewy grass.
A canvas rich in every hue,
As seasons gracefully pass.

Lavender whispers soft and low,
In a symphony of scents.
Each petal holds a tale to show,
In the dance of nature's intents.

Turquoise waters gently lap,
Merging colors, calm and flow.
Underneath a cozy lap,
The beauty of the world, aglow.

From the sky to ground below,
Every shade has its own role.
Nature's gems in vibrant show,
Together make a perfect whole.

Boughs Bearing the Weight of Whimsy

Boughs arch low with playful cheer,
Cradling dreams in each branch.
Whispered laughter fills the air,
In this enchanted, leafy ranch.

Birds weave tales of joy and flight,
As shadows dance on sunlit ground.
Each twig a canvas of delight,
Where the heart's pure bliss is found.

Swaying gently in sweet tunes,
The breeze sings softly through the trees.
Underneath the glow of moons,
Nature's melody brings ease.

Frolicking with sprites and fae,
Every leaf a secret shared.
In the twilight's gentle sway,
Each moment, beautifully bared.

As stars peek through the canopy,
The world feels light and free.
In whimsy wrapped, you'll see,
Nature's joyous jubilee.

Icy Murmurs in the Starlit Forest

Whispers glisten in the night,
Where frost clings to every bark.
Under starlight's silver light,
The forest holds its quiet spark.

Each breath a cloud of shimmering frost,
Time stands still in this cold embrace.
Echoes of the day are lost,
In the frosty, moonlit space.

Tall pines wear their icy crown,
As shadows dance with night's grace.
Softly, the world settles down,
In winter's soft, serene embrace.

Crystalline branches sway and sigh,
A lullaby of whispered dreams.
Underneath the vast night sky,
Nature glows with frosty beams.

In this realm, the stillness breathes,
Each snowflake a delicate art.
Icy murmurs share their pleas,
In the depths of a winter heart.

The Tangle of Seasons

Spring bursts forth in colors bright,
Fading whispers of winter's night.
Summer's heat begins to rise,
As autumn's chill draws nigh with sighs.

Branches sway in gentle dance,
Leaves collide in fleeting glance.
Time weaves through the vibrant thread,
A tapestry of life, we're led.

Nature's rhythm, pulse so strong,
In this tangle, we belong.
Each season plays its timeless part,
A circle drawn within the heart.

A Journey Through the Frosted Garden

In the hush of morning's light,
Frosted petals, pure and white.
Footsteps crunch on frozen ground,
Nature's silence all around.

Whispers of the winter breeze,
Kissing branches, swaying trees.
Each breath a cloud, a fleeting trace,
In this garden, time's embrace.

Mossy stones, a path so grand,
Guiding us through this quiet land.
A journey where the heart can soar,
Through beauty found forevermore.

Whispers of Winter's Embrace

Snowflakes dance in soft descent,
A world transformed, so pure, content.
Fires crackle, warmth surrounds,
In winter's hush, peace abounds.

Every star shines crystal clear,
Whispered secrets, drawing near.
Chilled air carries tales of old,
Wrapped in a silence, bold yet cold.

The moon hangs low, a silver globe,
Illuminating dreams untold.
In the stillness, hearts entwine,
Finding solace, sweet and mine.

Yuletide Spirit Beneath the Snow

Twinkling lights on branches bare,
Magic lingers in the air.
Carols sung with joy and cheer,
Yuletide spirit, drawing near.

Gifts wrapped small, love held tight,
Warmth of family in the night.
Hands held close, laughter shared,
In this season, hearts declared.

Beneath the snow, a glow so bright,
Dreams awakened, taking flight.
In the cold, our warmth will grow,
Yuletide spirit, soft as snow.

The Harmony of Leaf and Ice

In the whisper of the trees,
Leaves dance with the gentle breeze.
Crystal droplets fall like tears,
Nature's song, pure and clear.

Branches draped in winter's lace,
A fleeting moment, a tender grace.
Colors blend in twilight's glow,
A fusion only dreamers know.

Underneath the silver sky,
The world in stillness seems to sigh.
Life and frost in sweet embrace,
A harmony that time won't erase.

Every leaf, a memory caught,
In the cold, warmth's tender thought.
Together in this winter's maze,
They weave a tale that softly plays.

So pause and see this quiet truth,
In nature's heart, eternal youth.
The harmony of leaf and ice,
A serene world, a paradise.

A Palette of Winter's Breath

Brush strokes on a canvas white,
Winter paints with soft delight.
Subtle hues in silver blend,
A frosty beauty without end.

Every flake a work of art,
Nature's magic, a beating heart.
Whispered shades of blue and gray,
Winter's breath, a soft ballet.

The landscape dons a chilly hue,
Sparkling crystals, fresh and new.
Each moment frozen in its place,
Time suspended, a cool embrace.

Across the field, shadows play,
In the twilight, colors sway.
A palette rich in chilly air,
Each glance reveals a tale so rare.

In this serenity so deep,
Winter's promises gently creep.
A palette brushed with care and thought,
In every glance, a lesson taught.

Beauty Within the Frosted Frame

Glass panes covered in icy lace,
A frosted world, a silent grace.
In every corner, beauty glows,
Through a veil where stillness flows.

The gentle touch of winter's hand,
Shapes each miracle, each strand.
Brittle whispers, soft and light,
Frame a scene of purest white.

A crystal garden, silent and fair,
Nature's wonders hanging there.
In every shimmer, lives a dream,
Reflections caught in frozen beam.

Within the frost, the warmth resides,
In quiet spots where hope abides.
Beauty captured in every line,
A frosted frame, a love divine.

So stand awhile and take it in,
The beauty where the cold begins.
In every breath, a quiet claim,
Life within the frosted frame.

The Cradle of Icy Elegance

Nestled deep in winter's hold,
A cradle wrapped in stories told.
Each flake a note of whispered charm,
Embracing earth in gentle calm.

Layers soft as dreams at night,
Guide the stars with muted light.
Elegance in silver stream,
A frozen world, a tranquil dream.

Curved branches bow with grace,
Nature's beauty finds its place.
In the hush, a secret prayer,
For warmth that lingers in the air.

A soulless winter, tender yet,
Within its heart, our hopes are set.
Icy elegance, pure and bright,
The cradle holds both day and night.

So linger here, where moments weave,
A tapestry that we believe.
In the cradle of icy grace,
A world awash in love's embrace.

Frigid Gardens in the Embrace of Celebration

In gardens where the frost does creep,
Lights dance softly, secrets keep.
Joyous laughter fills the air,
As whispers float, a festive prayer.

Beneath the stars, the colors gleam,
Each petal caught in winter's dream.
Children play in snowy mounds,
While love and cheer in hearts abound.

The trees adorned in icy lace,
Reflect the warmth of every face.
Celebration echoes bright,
In the chill of winter's night.

Candles flicker, warmth prevails,
Through frozen paths, the spirit sails.
Together we sing, hand in hand,
In this frigid, joyous land.

Hope springs eternal, the heart ignites,
In gardens kissed by shimmering lights.
Each moment cherished, memories made,
In the embrace of love, we wade.

Shining Secrets of the Frozen Hearth

By the hearth, a fire glows,
Whispers of the past it knows.
Shadows dance on frosty walls,
As time stands still in winter's thralls.

Every ember tells a tale,
Of joy and sorrow, soft and frail.
Golden warmth against the cold,
In the quiet, secrets unfold.

Snowflakes drift like gentle dreams,
Catching light in silver streams.
With each flicker, spirits rise,
Underneath the starlit skies.

In the comfort of this space,
Frozen moments find their grace.
Hope ignites, luminous and bright,
At the hearth, the heart takes flight.

Together we gather, hand in hand,
In the glow of warmth, we stand.
Shining stories, bright and clear,
In the frozen hush, we draw near.

Joyful Journeys Through the Snow-kissed Woods

Through woodlands draped in silken white,
Every step a dance of light.
Joyful laughter fills the air,
As footprints whisper everywhere.

Snowflakes flutter, nature's grace,
Transforming every hidden space.
Together we tread the winding paths,
Embracing joy; no room for wrath.

With every breath, the crispness sings,
Bringing warmth as the heart takes wings.
In the snowfall's gentle cradle,
Adventure calls us to this fable.

The trees are crowned with icy dreams,
Reflecting soft, celestial beams.
Every turn, a story waits,
In the woods where joy elates.

As daylight fades, the stars appear,
Guiding us through paths sincere.
In joyful journeys, hand in hand,
We find magic in winter's land.

Echoes of Yuletide in Silent Scenes

In silent scenes where spirits soar,
Yuletide echoes, forevermore.
Softly falls the glistening snow,
Wrapping the world in a peaceful glow.

Carols hum in the frosty air,
Each note a balm, dispelling care.
Underneath the starry spread,
The whispers of hope gently tread.

Candles flicker, shadows play,
Reflecting on this sacred day.
Memories linger, warmly bound,
In the hush where love is found.

A gathering of hearts so dear,
In every laugh, we conquer fear.
United in this tender space,
We cherish blessings time can't erase.

As night descends with gentle grace,
The spirit of joy we embrace.
In echoes of Yuletide's gleam,
We live our dreams within this theme.

A Twinkle of Warmth in Crisp Air

In the bite of morning's zest,
Sunrise paints the sky anew,
A twinkle hugs the world so close,
While frost-kissed whispers dance and skew.

Footsteps crunch on powdered ground,
As laughter echoes through the trees,
With every breath, a cloud unbound,
The chill submits to joyous ease.

Scarves wrapped tight and cheeks aglow,
Hot cocoa warms the shivering hands,
We gather close, our hearts in tow,
Painting dreams like winter strands.

Embers flicker in the night,
Stars peek out from velvet skies,
Their twinkling warmth, a soft delight,
As moonlit secrets softly rise.

So let us treasure fleeting days,
When warmth and chill entwine like art,
For in this dance of light's embrace,
We find the glow within the heart.

Nature's Artistry in the Deep Chill

Beneath the frost, the earth does sleep,
Blanketed in snow's soft sigh,
Nature's brush paints visions deep,
In wintry hues that never die.

A canvas wide, the trees stand bare,
Glittering crystals catch the sun,
Each branch adorned with perfect flair,
A masterpiece of cold, well done.

Silence rules this tranquil scene,
Except for whispers of the breeze,
A symphony of white unseen,
In nature's grip, our souls find ease.

With every flake that tumbles down,
A dance of beauty, light and free,
Each moment fleeting, like a crown,
Worn by winter's majesty.

So pause and breathe, behold the art,
In every shadow, every light,
For nature's touch, it is the heart,
Of winter's breath, wrapped in delight.

Calm Resilience Beneath a Glittering Veil

Amidst the storm, there's quiet grace,
A resilience that runs so deep,
Beneath the cloak of winter's embrace,
The heart beats softly, strong, not weak.

Each flake that falls, a gentle note,
Sings stories of the brave and bold,
In layers thick where dreams do float,
Life pulses bright, defying cold.

With every gust, a soft reply,
Branches sway in rhythmic cheer,
The world may freeze, yet hearts can fly,
In the silence, love draws near.

The stars perch high, a guiding light,
Their glitter sparkles on the snow,
In darkness blooms a hope so bright,
As whispers of warmth gently flow.

So stand and feel the winter's breath,
Know calm resilience is our way,
For in this dance, life conquers death,
In every moment, seize the day.

Enigmatic Hues Across the White Canvas

A canvas vast, so pure, so wide,
Strokes of color in silence blend,
Nature's secret, a love-tied ride,
In every corner, hues transcend.

Lavenders bloom where shadows play,
While arctic blues and greens commandeer,
A vibrant tapestry on display,
In whispers soft, the heart grows near.

Golden glimmers in frozen streams,
Reflecting dreams of warmer days,
In nature's brush, vivid schemes,
Of life revived in brilliant ways.

The dancing auroras swirl and weave,
With every flicker, spirits lift,
In this enchantment, we believe,
That winter holds a magic gift.

So let us wander through this space,
And feel the brush of winter's care,
For in the chill, a warm embrace,
Awaits in hues, beyond compare.

Lush Memories Encased in White

Snowflakes dance and swirl anew,
Covering all in a blanket of hue.
Whispers of warmth in frozen air,
Echoes of laughter, memories rare.

Branches bow with glistening grace,
Time stands still in this quiet space.
Footprints left in the pristine white,
Moments captured, a pure delight.

Fires crackle with gentle glow,
Stories shared as embers flow.
In winter's grasp, hearts intertwine,
Lush memories in icy design.

An Ode to Scarlet Against the Grey

Amidst the fog, a vibrant flare,
Petals plunge through the heavy air.
A scarlet bloom, defiant and bold,
In a world of grey, a story unfolds.

Leaves turn soft with a whispering sigh,
While shadows gather, and sunbeams cry.
The red persists, a radiant light,
Challenging dusk to embrace the night.

Colors clash in a fierce ballet,
Life's canvas painted in disarray.
A fleeting moment, yet fierce and free,
An ode to scarlet, a symphony.

Glimmering Dreams Under the Icy Sky

Stars twinkle in the velvet night,
Whispers of dreams take fragile flight.
Beneath the frost, a world awakes,
In glistening silence, the heart breaks.

Moonlight spills on the frozen ground,
Shadows dance without a sound.
Visions shimmer in winter's embrace,
Soft, fleeting dreams in tranquil space.

Nature's breath, a chilly sigh,
Echoes of fate beneath the sky.
In crystal realms where wishes fly,
Glimmering dreams, and hopes set high.

The Last Whisper of Autumn

Leaves cascade in a golden swirl,
Autumn's breath begins to unfurl.
The trees stand tall, yet softly bow,
Bidding farewell to the time endows.

Crisp air tinged with earth's sweet spice,
Harvest moon glows, a soft advice.
Time trickles into the past's embrace,
The last whisper in nature's grace.

Colors fade as the chill creeps near,
Memories linger, tender and clear.
A season's close, yet life persists,
In the heart of change, we still exist.

Beneath the Crystal Canopy

Underneath the shimmering sky,
Whispers of the night do sigh.
Stars are wrapped in silver light,
Dreams take flight, like birds in flight.

Branches glisten, softly sway,
Nature's dance will never fray.
Moonbeams kiss the tranquil stream,
In the dark, we weave a dream.

Secrets bold the shadows keep,
While the world drifts fast asleep.
Crickets sing a lullaby,
To the night that draws us nigh.

Gentle breezes stir the leaves,
In this space, the heart believes.
Beneath the canopy of stars,
Life unfolds, and love is ours.

Memories twinkle in the night,
Golden moments, pure delight.
Beneath this crystal, endless dome,
In nature's heart, we find our home.

The Gift of Ice and Ember

In the stillness of the morn,
Glistening frost, the world reborn.
Ice crystals sparkle, diamonds fair,
Morning whispers through the air.

Embers glow from fireside bright,
Warming souls against the night.
Each flicker tells of love's embrace,
In the dance of time and space.

Snowflakes drift like tiny dreams,
Falling softly, gentle seams.
Nature paints in hues of white,
Transforming day from dark to light.

With each step on frozen ground,
Echoes of the past resound.
Hands entwined, we brave the chill,
The union of our hearts fulfilled.

Together, we sail through the cold,
Holding on to tales retold.
In this realm of fire and ice,
We find joy, we pay the price.

Glades of Brilliance

Sunlight dances on the grass,
Through the glade, let moments pass.
Colors burst in wild array,
Nature sings in bright display.

Breezes carry floral scents,
Each petal holds a world immense.
In the hush of afternoon,
Life awakens to its tune.

Deer are grazing, calm and free,
Whispered secrets, just for me.
A brook bubbles with delight,
Reflecting dreams in morning light.

Time stands still as shadows blend,
In this space, all hearts mend.
Beneath the boughs that gently sway,
We discover new pathways.

Glades of brilliance call us near,
In this haven, void of fear.
Every step is full of grace,
A journey through this sacred place.

A Jewel among the Drifts

Amidst the snow, a jewel glows,
Sparkling bright where the cold wind blows.
Each flake dances, soft and sweet,
Nature's canvas where dreams meet.

Winter's breath is crisp and clear,
Treasures hidden, drawing near.
In the silence, echoes ring,
Stories told of love and spring.

Footprints etched in frosty ground,
Travelers lost but then found.
Every turn holds magic bright,
In the depths of winter's night.

A moment savored, time stands still,
Hearts are warmed against the chill.
A jewel found in nature's embrace,
Forever cherished, a sacred place.

So we wander through the light,
Finding joy in the purest sight.
Among the drifts, our spirits soar,
In this wonderland, forevermore.

The Radiance of Holiday's Touch

In the glow of evening's light,
Fires crackle, spirits bright.
Joyful laughter fills the air,
Warm embraces, love to share.

Gifts wrapped in colors bold,
Stories of the past retold.
Hearts aglow with pure delight,
Chasing shadows of the night.

Carols sung in harmony,
Whispers of sweet memory.
Hope and peace, a gentle guide,
In this season, love won't hide.

With every toast, a wish is made,
Unity in moments stayed.
To cherish those who gather near,
The magic of this time is clear.

As the stars appear above,
We are wrapped in warmth and love.
In the radiance of this touch,
Life's simple gifts, we cherish much.

Enchantment of the Silent Night

Moonlight dances on the snow,
Whispers secrets, soft and low.
Stars blink down with quiet grace,
In this calm, we find our place.

Shadows linger, dreams take flight,
Fires flicker, hearts feel light.
Silence wraps the world in peace,
In this moment, all fears cease.

Footsteps crunch on frosty ground,
In the stillness, magic found.
Nature holds its breath in awe,
Revelations, life's gentle law.

Here beneath the vast expanse,
We surrender to this chance.
To reflect, to feel, to see,
In the night, we find our key.

Enchantment glows in every heart,
Silent night, a work of art.
In the shadows, love ignites,
In the stillness, joy takes flight.

Twinkling Lights on Frost-kissed Pines

Twinkling lights adorn the trees,
Dancing softly with the breeze.
Frost-kissed branches shine so bright,
An enchanting, wondrous sight.

As the night unfolds its quilt,
Every heart with wonder built.
Magic whispers through the air,
In each corner, love laid bare.

Children's laughter fills the space,
Excitement draws a smiling face.
With each glow, the world feels right,
Guided by these stars alight.

Gathered close in warmth and cheer,
Treasured moments held so dear.
Songs of joy and hope resound,
In this beauty, bliss is found.

Shimmering dreams in every heart,
From this light, we cannot part.
With soft glows that intertwine,
We find peace in frosted pines.

A Heartwarming Chill in the Air

Winter whispers in the chill,
Frosty nights that time stands still.
Scarves wrapped snug, we wander near,
Moments shared with those we cheer.

Breath of fog upon the night,
Candles flicker, spirits bright.
All around, a frosty gleam,
In our hearts, we hold a dream.

Traces of the past appear,
Echoes of friends drawing near.
Laughter dances, warm like fire,
Embers spark our heart's desire.

Cups of cocoa, steaming hot,
In the stillness, joy is caught.
Every hug, a treasured gift,
In this season, spirits lift.

With each step in winter's embrace,
Love's reminder, time and space.
Feel the chill, let troubles fade,
In the warmth of memories made.

Chilly Echoes of Nature's Warmth

The whispering winds begin to swell,
While leaves dance lightly, stories tell.
A sunbeam breaks through the frosty air,
Revealing warmth, a gentle flare.

Snowflakes twirl in a vibrant dance,
Nature's magic, a fleeting chance.
Footprints linger on a path once bright,
Chilly echoes fade into night.

Crystals sparkle on evergreen bows,
Inviting awe from nature's vows.
Each breath a cloud in the crisp embrace,
Chilly echoes in a warm place.

A moment captured, so pure and clear,
Nature's heartbeat, ever near.
With a tender kiss from the winter sun,
Chilly echoes, two worlds as one.

Frosted Invitations to Merriment

A blanket of white, a pure delight,
Frosted whispers in morning light.
Joyful laughter fills the air,
Inviting all to winter's fair.

Children bundle, cheeks aglow,
Snowball fights and laughter flow.
Skates carve paths on a frozen pond,
Frosted invitations, life beyond.

Hot cocoa steaming, marshmallows play,
Warmth envelops at end of day.
Friends gather 'round with cheer instilled,
Frosted moments, hearts fulfilled.

The fire crackles, stories rise,
Under a canvas of moonlit skies.
With every whisper, winter calls,
Frosted invitations in silent halls.

A Tale of Green Beneath the Silver Sky

Beneath the silver, clouds drift and glide,
Emerald hills and valleys wide.
A tale unfolds, so lush and bright,
Nature's canvas, a wondrous sight.

Gentle streams weave through the land,
Whispers of life, a touch of sand.
Buds awaken, as blossoms bloom,
A tale of green dispels the gloom.

Mountains loom in shadows tall,
Silent witnesses to nature's call.
Sunset paints with strokes of gold,
A tale retold, forever bold.

Together we breathe this lively air,
With every heartbeat, without a care.
Nature thrives beneath the heavenly dome,
A tale of green forever at home.

Chilling Elegance of Nature's Palette

Brush strokes of frost on winter's breath,
Nature's palette, a dance of death.
Silvery hues on branches stark,
Chilling elegance in the dark.

Whirls of snow in a graceful flight,
Each flake unique, a fleeting sight.
Moonlight shimmers, a diamond view,
Chilling elegance in the blue.

Whispered secrets in the quiet night,
The world transformed, a pure delight.
Stars twinkle softly, twined in mist,
Chilling elegance too good to resist.

Winds softly weave through shadows long,
Carrying whispers of nature's song.
A symphony played in silence true,
Chilling elegance painted anew.

Blossoms of Resilience in Winter's Grip

In the chill of silence vast,
Petals brave, they hold steadfast.
Through the frost, they push and fight,
Color bursts in pale moonlight.

Buds that bloom in starkest cold,
Stories of the brave retold.
Roots entangled, deep and true,
Whispers soft of life anew.

Nature's dance, a steadfast sway,
Turning night into the day.
Hope resides in every branch,
With the thaw, they take their chance.

Each frozen tear sustains them well,
In the heart where stories dwell.
Forging through the starkest pain,
Their existence, a fierce gain.

Blossoms shining, pure and bright,
In the bleak, they bring the light.
Winter's grasp will fade away,
Strength in beauty, come what may.

Gemstone Hues of Nature's Serenity

Emerald leaves in gentle sway,
Underneath the sun's warm play.
Rivers flow in sapphire streams,
Whispers soft of waking dreams.

Amber skies at dusk unfold,
Stories of the day retold.
Crimson blooms in fields of green,
Nature's palette, pure and clean.

Lavender clouds in twilight's haze,
Kissing earth in sunset's blaze.
Serenity in every hue,
Life's bright colors, ever true.

Golden rays that touch the ground,
Harmony in all around.
With gemstone lights, the world will gleam,
In nature's heart, we find our dream.

Crystal droplets on the leaves,
Nature's breath, it gently weaves.
A symphony of colors blend,
In this peace, our hearts ascend.

Whirlwinds of Festivity in the Frost

Snowflakes dance in frosty air,
Joyous laughter everywhere.
Children's voices, pure delight,
Sparkling eyes against the night.

Bonfires crackling, warmth aglow,
Tales of cheer and hearts in tow.
Merriment beneath the stars,
Frosty breath and open cars.

Twinkling lights on every street,
Echoing the joy we meet.
Spinning through the winter's chill,
In our hearts, the fire fills.

Glowing candles, wishes made,
In each moment, memories laid.
Whirlwinds swirling, festive flair,
Wrapping joy in winter's air.

Frosty mornings, hot cocoa treat,
Gathering where all friends meet.
In the cold, our spirits rise,
Whirlwinds bright beneath the skies.

Enchanted Greens Against Crystal White

In the forest's deep embrace,
Emerald life finds its place.
Among the white, so bold and bright,
Nature's canvas, pure delight.

Mossy beds on frozen ground,
In the silence, peace is found.
Pines adorned with frosty lace,
Magic drapes in every space.

Whispers of the winter breeze,
Rustle softly through the trees.
Every branch, a tale is spun,
Life persists in winter's fun.

Golden light through foliage streams,
Where the heart flows with the dreams.
In the stillness, life ignites,
Enchanted greens in snowy nights.

Crisp and clear, the world feels new,
Every shadow kissed by dew.
Against the white, they stretch and grow,
Nature's wonder, in the snow.

Shimmering Leaves Within the Crystal

In the twilight, leaves ignite,
With shimmering hues, pure delight.
Glistening softly, in the breeze,
Nature whispers, 'Feel at ease.'

Crystals sparkle, sunlight plays,
Wrapped in warmth of autumn days.
Golden edges, crisp and fair,
A dance of colors, everywhere.

Through the branches, shadows prance,
In the woods, a fleeting chance.
Memories twirl, caught in flight,
Lost in the magic of the night.

Amongst the whispers, secrets call,
Underneath the leaves, we fall.
A heartbeat echoes, time stands still,
In the crystal light, I feel the thrill.

Nature's palette, vibrant, bold,
Stories of the earth retold.
A glimmering promise, pure and true,
Within these leaves, I find my view.

The Serene Dance of Winter's Glow

In the stillness, snowflakes sway,
Beneath the moon, they gently play.
Blankets white, all around,
In this hush, serenity found.

Whispers of frost kiss the night,
Stars above twinkle with delight.
A frozen stream, sparkling bright,
Nature's wonder, purest light.

Branches glisten, nature's crown,
Softly draping, winter gown.
A tranquil moment, pure and clear,
In the silence, peace draws near.

Footsteps crunch on snow's embrace,
Every path a gentle trace.
In this dance of night and day,
Magic lingers, come what may.

Winter's breath, a whispered song,
In its embrace, we all belong.
Warmth of hearth, a glowing cheer,
In this season, love is near.

Evergreen Dreams in a Winter Wonderland

Evergreen trees stand tall and proud,
Draped in snow, beneath a shroud.
In the forest, silence sings,
Wrapped in warmth of winter's wings.

Frozen pathways, trails of white,
Sparkling under morning light.
In the whispers, dreams take flight,
Magic dances through the night.

Glistening branches, nature's crown,
Holding secrets deep, profound.
As the chill wraps all around,
In this wonderland, joy is found.

Children laughing, snowflakes chase,
Creating memories in this space.
In the air, anticipation grows,
Evergreen dreams, where love bestows.

Fires crackle, hearts will bloom,
In this splendor, winter's room.
Cozy moments, stories shared,
Evergreen dreams, always cared.

A Sprinkle of Yuletide Magic

In the air, a sweet scent swirls,
Festive lights and laughter curls.
Joyous carols fill the night,
A sprinkle of magic, pure delight.

Chimneys puffing, warmth inside,
Stars above, a cosmic guide.
In the hearth, the flames do dance,
In this moment, hearts entrance.

Gifts wrapped gently, ribbons tied,
Stories shared, and hearts open wide.
A cup of cheer, friends gather near,
With a sprinkle of love, we hold dear.

Snowflakes drifting, soft and light,
Covering the world, pure and white.
In the twinkle of the tree,
Magic whispers to you and me.

As we cherish, memories blend,
In this season, love transcends.
A sprinkle of joy, forever lasts,
In our hearts, the magic casts.

Frigid Petals Under Moonlit Skies

Frigid petals softly cling,
To the night's cool, gentle breath.
Moonlit skies respond and sing,
Whispers of the night's bequest.

In the stillness, shadows dance,
Casting dreams on purest white.
Every moment, given chance,
Bears the magic of the night.

Stars above, like silver threads,
Stitch the fabric of our gaze.
Underneath where silence spreads,
Time unwinds in softest ways.

Frozen blossoms, spirits bright,
Glimmers caught in tender glow.
Nature's charm in crisp moonlight,
Where the frost and beauty flow.

As the dawn begins to break,
Frigid petals start to fade.
In the beauty, hearts awake,
Memories of night conveyed.

The Berry-laden Boughs of December

Berry-laden boughs so low,
In winter's chill, they gleam like fire.
Nature's bounty, bright in snow,
Fruits of labor, hearts inspire.

Crimson clusters, sweet delight,
Whispering secrets to the cold.
In the stillness of the night,
Tales of warmth and love retold.

Branches heavy, drinks of cheer,
Laden dreams in frosty air.
Echoes of the season near,
Breath of life in winter's glare.

Underneath the moon's soft glance,
Hopes awaken, birds take flight.
In the quiet, nature's dance,
Berry-laden boughs ignite.

As December winds do blow,
You can find a warmth inside.
Cherished moments start to grow,
With each heartbeat, joy and pride.

A Tapestry of Frosted Whispers

A tapestry of frost behold,
Whispers spun on icy lace.
Every thread a story told,
In the chill, a still embrace.

Snowflakes fall like dreams in flight,
Kissing earth with softest grace.
Underneath the pale moonlight,
Nature's wonders interlace.

Gentle echoes, secrets shared,
In the silence, soft and clear.
Amidst the frost, we're ensnared,
In this realm, no need for fear.

Every shimmer, every gleam,
Crafts a world of pure delight.
In the heart, a timeless dream,
Wrapped in whispers of the night.

As the dawn breaks, beauty fades,
Yet the memories will remain.
Frosted whispers serenade,
In our hearts, a sweet refrain.

Chilling Reveries in Evergreen Glades

Chilling reveries unfold,
In the depths of evergreen.
Nature's secrets softly told,
In the hush, a hidden sheen.

Whispers weave through branches tall,
Gentle breezes kiss the ground.
In the echo, hear the call,
Of forgotten dreams unbound.

Evergreen, a timeless phase,
Guardian of winter's grace.
In the stillness, quiet plays,
Songs of warmth in cold embrace.

In the glades where shadows shift,
Mysteries awaken still.
Nature's touch, a precious gift,
Filling hearts with joy at will.

As the twilight paints the trees,
With a brush of softest white,
Chilling reveries like these,
Guide us gently to the night.

Silent Nights of Vibrant Memories

Silent nights whisper dreams,
Stars twinkle with glee,
Echoes of laughter linger,
As we sip on warm tea.

The moon bathes the snow,
In a soft, silver glow,
Footprints trail behind us,
Where only the brave go.

Crackling fireside tales,
Wrap us in their light,
Moments freeze in time,
Held close through the night.

Old songs fill the air,
Singing of times past,
With every note we dance,
In memories that last.

As dawn breaks the spell,
Colors burst anew,
Yet in the heart we hold,
The night's magic too.

Glistening Garlands and Frosty Refrains

Glistening garlands hung high,
On branches wrapped in white,
Frosty refrains fill the air,
In harmony with the night.

Golden lights start to twinkle,
Casting shadows on the ground,
While laughter dances softly,
In moments we have found.

Snowflakes drift like whispers,
A tapestry so fine,
We bundle close together,
As warmth begins to shine.

Chilly winds may blow fierce,
But hearts are snug and warm,
Tales of joy and friendship,
Reveal winter's charm.

With each breath of the night,
Hope lingers in the air,
Glistening garlands brighten,
Every moment we share.

Winter's Embrace of Timeless Joy

In winter's soft embrace,
Nature finds its rest,
Blankets of white silence,
Cradle every quest.

Timeless joy surrounds us,
In games of snow and play,
With each laugh that echoes,
We chase the cold away.

Eager hearts explore,
The frosted, open fields,
As whispers of the year,
A gentle warmth reveals.

Stars alight the heavens,
Guide us through the night,
While cozy hearts remember,
What makes our spirits bright.

Savor every moment,
In winter's gentle hold,
For joy is found in memories,
As the beauty unfolds.

Jewel-toned Spirits in the Cold

Jewel-toned spirits glimmer,
Against the evening sky,
Frosted air enchanted,
As the stars drift by.

Crimson, green, and azure,
Colors swirl and dance,
In the hush of chilly nights,
We find our hearts' romance.

The warmth of fires crackles,
With stories all around,
In each jewel-toned flicker,
New adventures can be found.

Beneath the icy blanket,
Life waits to re-emerge,
With every breath of winter,
Hope begins to surge.

So let us raise our glasses,
To friends, both near and far,
In this season of wonder,
Shining like a star.

The Song of Frostbitten Flora

Beneath the frost, the petals lie,
Their colors muted, a silent sigh.
Yet in the chill, resilience glows,
A tale of beauty that winter bestows.

Amidst the snow, the stems stand tall,
In icy grasp, they heed the call.
With every breath, they sing their song,
A melody pure, where they belong.

The air is crisp, the world is still,
Nature whispers with a gentle thrill.
From frozen ground, life yearns to break,
A symphony waking, for spring's sweet sake.

Though winter's breath is sharp and cold,
Each frostbitten flower holds dreams untold.
In frigid gardens, magic resides,
As hope and warmth in silence abides.

So let us cherish this bracing sight,
The song of flora, a dance of light.
For even in frost, life finds a way,
To bloom anew at the break of day.

Winter's Bounty on Boughs of Joy

A tapestry woven on branches bare,
Crystals of ice in the frosty air.
Each bough adorned, a shimmering hue,
Nature's harvest, a splendid view.

The weight of snow like a gentle embrace,
Cocooning life in a tranquil space.
In this stillness, the world transforms,
As winter's bounty takes various forms.

Glittering lights on the tree's outspread,
Whispering secrets of warmth ahead.
Though cold winds blow, the heart ignites,
With every glance, winter delights.

As twilight approaches, shadows fall,
Yet beauty lingers, answering the call.
In the embrace of winter's chill,
The joy of nature brings warmth still.

So let us raise a glass, rejoice,
In winter's bounty, we find our voice.
For every flake that descends from the sky,
Promises of joy, like stars up high.

Glistening Whispers of the Season

The trees are wrapped in diamond lace,
As winter whispers in every place.
A hush envelops the world outside,
In the chilly breath, all dreams abide.

With every flake that softly lands,
A glistening silence, as nature stands.
In the delicate grasp of every sigh,
A whispered promise of days gone by.

The sun peeks through, a timid friend,
Its rays a glimmer, a warmth to lend.
In shadows long, the magic grows,
With every moment, the wonder flows.

As night falls soft, the stars appear,
Lighting the skies, drawing us near.
In winter's embrace, we find our peace,
A soothing balm, where worries cease.

So let us dance in the frosty air,
With glistening whispers everywhere.
For in this season, the heart finds grace,
In every corner, a sacred space.

The Promise of Green in Icebound Dreams

Beneath the frost, a whisper stirs,
In dreams of green, the life confers.
The earth is sleeping, but hope will rise,
In the thawing warmth of clearer skies.

With icy breath, the world is still,
Yet somewhere deep, resides a thrill.
For every seed that rests in slumber,
The promise of green begins to encumber.

As winter fades, with gentle hands,
The ice will melt, as spring commands.
From snow to bloom, the cycle turns,
In heart and soil, a fire burns.

Each droplet's fall, each ray of light,
Will coax the earth to leave the night.
With vibrant hues, the world will gleam,
Awakening from icebound dream.

So revel in this fleeting chill,
For green shall come, and hearts will fill.
In every whisper, let hope resound,
For spring is coming, life unbound.

Wreaths of Nature's Elegance

In meadows green, the blossoms sway,
With gentle breath, they greet the day.
A tapestry of hues displayed,
Nature's grace in every shade.

Among the trees, the whispers call,
Each leaf a story, grand and small.
The dance of shadows, light's embrace,
Wreaths of life, a soft, warm grace.

A stream flows clear, reflecting skies,
Beneath the branches, beauty lies.
The symphony of the softest sound,
In nature's arms, our hearts are found.

As seasons change, the colors merge,
From bloom to fade, the life will surge.
In every petal, the earth's delight,
Wreaths of nature in gentle flight.

A canvas painted by the sun,
Each stroke a gift, a day begun.
With every breath, a promise made,
In nature's arms, we'll never fade.

Snow-kissed Glamour

Soft snowflakes fall, a glistening sight,
Covering earth in shimmering white.
Each crystal sparkles in warm embrace,
A winter's hush, a calm, sweet grace.

The trees wear coats of frosty lace,
Branches bowed low in a gentle trace.
Footprints mark the path we tread,
In a dreamscape where magic is spread.

Under street lamps, shadows play,
As twilight fades to end the day.
The world transformed, so pure and bright,
Snow-kissed moments, pure delight.

Whispers of wind through frosty air,
Every breath held without a care.
In silence deep, the heartbeats thrum,
As winter's charm begins to hum.

Together we laugh, our spirits high,
Flinging snowballs, letting joy fly.
With every smile, we find the glow,
In the magic of the snow-kissed show.

The Echoes of Solstice

When shadows lengthen, the light grows dim,
The fading sun, a haunting hymn.
In twilight's hold, the stars ignite,
Whispers of dreams in the deepening night.

The solstice sings with a solemn grace,
Revealing paths in the cosmic space.
As seasons shift, the tides shall turn,
In ancient echoes, the lanterns burn.

A dance of fireflies in twilight's hold,
Each flicker tells of stories old.
Unraveled threads of time's embrace,
In every shadow, the past we trace.

With every dawn, new beginnings bloom,
Life awakens from winter's gloom.
Yet in the silence, a tale unfolds,
The echoes call with whispers bold.

Within the night, our hearts unite,
In the chorus of the celestial flight.
As earth renews under starlit skies,
The echoes of solstice softly rise.

Scarlet Blooms Beneath Glaze

In the garden, the scarlet blooms,
Bursting forth like joyous grooms.
Petals vibrant against the grey,
A beacon bright on winter's day.

Beneath the frost, their colors sigh,
Defying cold, they reach for sky.
With every petal, a story told,
Of warmth and sun in glimmers bold.

The year's end brings a fleeting grace,
As nature dons her icy lace.
Yet in this chill, there's hope aglow,
Scarlet blooms amidst the snow.

They whisper tales of springtime's kiss,
A promise held in frozen bliss.
With every breath, their essence stays,
Scarlet blooms beneath the glaze.

In twilight's hush, they softly gleam,
Reflecting dreams, a vibrant theme.
In winter's grasp, beauty will rise,
Scarlet blooms, our heart's reprise.

Boughs Adorned with Nature's Treasures

Boughs adorned with vibrant hues,
Golden leaves in autumn's muse.
Whispers soft in gentle breeze,
Nature's gift, a thousand keys.

Birdsongs weave a lullaby,
Underneath the sprawling sky.
In the woods, enchantments stir,
Life's embrace, a tender blur.

Through the branches, sunlight plays,
Dancing shadows, warm sunrays.
Every rustle, every sound,
In this haven, peace is found.

Boughs adorned, a sight to see,
Nature's art, wild and free.
In the quiet, hearts can soar,
Endless wonders to explore.

Time stands still where dreams reside,
In the forest, hopes abide.
Boughs adorned, spirits rise,
Underneath these painted skies.

The Color of Silence

The color of silence falls like snow,
Soft and gentle, a peaceful flow.
Whispers hidden in the air,
Quiet moments beyond compare.

In the dusk, where shadows blend,
Time will pause, and stillness mend.
Blue and gray, a tranquil scene,
Echoing thoughts, serene and keen.

Night enfolds with velvet grace,
Crickets sing in soft embrace.
Moonlight glimmers on the ground,
In this space, solace found.

Colors dim, yet hearts ignite,
In the silence, pure delight.
Every breath a note of peace,
In this hush, all worries cease.

The color of silence, pure and true,
Wraps the world in a soothing hue.
Listen closely, hear the call,
In the silence, love for all.

Starlit Trails Under the Glaze

Starlit trails beneath the night,
Whispers soft in silver light.
Moonbeams dance on velvet skies,
Guiding dreams where magic lies.

Pathways woven with gentle grace,
Every step, a quiet trace.
In the stillness, secrets grow,
Nature's wonders on full show.

Constellations tell their tales,
Journeying through cosmic trails.
Hearts aligned with every star,
Finding peace, no matter how far.

Starlit trails where wishes bloom,
Filling every heart with room.
For the dreams that silently chase,
In the night, we find our place.

Under the glaze, we roam free,
Bound by light and destiny.
In the dark, connections rise,
Starlit trails, where courage lies.

Echoing Lullabies of Winter

Echoing lullabies of winter's breath,
Whispers of wonder in moments left.
Snowflakes dance, a soft embrace,
Blanketing earth in delicate lace.

Fires crackle, warmth draws near,
Hearts entwined, joy sincere.
In the quiet, stories weave,
Tales of love that we believe.

Winter's chill, but spirits bright,
Glimmers of hope in the long night.
Every flake, a tale to tell,
In the peace, we find our spell.

Echoing lullabies softly play,
Carrying dreams on winter's sway.
Snowy wonderland, pure delight,
In the silence, hearts take flight.

Through the frost, together we sing,
Embracing warmth that love can bring.
Echoing lullabies fill the air,
In winter's arms, we find our care.

Gleaming Boughs of Red

In autumn's light, they dance and sway,
Gleaming boughs of red on display.
Whispers of leaves, soft serenade,
Nature's canvas, a vibrant parade.

Beneath the trees, the shadows play,
Crimson hues chase the gray away.
Rustling softly, the wind does call,
A symphony sung by the woods so tall.

Frigid Dreams and Scarlet Gleams

In winter's clutch, the world turns white,
Frigid dreams in the pale moonlight.
Scarlet gleams on the frozen streams,
Where silence lingers and hope redeems.

The frosty breath of the night is near,
Each breath I take, crystal clear.
Beneath the stars, I find my way,
In dreams of warmth, I long to stay.

Verdant Secrets in White

Spring whispered soft, her secrets unfold,
Verdant secrets tucked in the cold.
In blankets of white, life stirs anew,
Each bud a promise, each leaf a view.

Among the blooms, joy starts to rise,
In hues of green beneath bright skies.
Nature awakens with gentle grace,
A tender touch on a sleeping face.

The Frosted Whisper

In quiet woods, a whisper flows,
The frosted air, a tale bestows.
Each twig adorned with jewels of ice,
A shimmering world, so pure and nice.

As dawn breaks forth, the light will gleam,
Chasing the night, a golden dream.
Nature's breath in a gentle sigh,
Whispers of frost, beneath the sky.

Heartbeats Beneath the Ice

Underneath the frozen lake,
Whispers of warmth gently quake.
Silent dreams in quiet sighs,
Pulse of love before it dies.

Frosty fingers touch the soul,
Seeking out the hidden whole.
In the stillness, hearts collide,
Finding shelter deep inside.

Footprints trace a path of fate,
Each heartbeat, a gentle state.
Beneath the ice, where shadows grow,
Life awaits the spring's soft glow.

Crystalline tears start to form,
Fleeting moments, fierce and warm.
Under starlit skies we dream,
Hope unfurls, a radiant beam.

Nature's blanket, pure and white,
Cocooned warmth in endless night.
Heartbeats echo, soft and clear,
Binding souls who linger near.

A Siren's Call in the Cold

Beneath the snow, a voice will rise,
Calling softly, 'See the skies!'
Melodies dance on crisp, clear air,
A siren's charm, both sweet and rare.

Echoed laughter, pure delight,
In the stillness of the night.
Frigid waters hide the sound,
Tempting hearts that dare to drown.

Whispers echo, secrets told,
Promises wrapped in icy cold.
Out to sea, the currents flow,
Drawing in those who long to know.

Trapped in dreams of glimmering ice,
Choosing love comes with a price.
Yet the pull is hard to fight,
A siren's call, a shivering light.

Stars above begin to gleam,
Casting shadows that make us dream.
In the distance, waves will break,
A siren's wake, for hearts to take.

The Sway of Icy Branches

Icy branches gently sway,
Whispering secrets of the day.
Crystals sparkle, catching light,
A frozen dance ignites the night.

Swaying softly in the breeze,
Nature's grace puts minds at ease.
Beneath the weight of winter's quilt,
A fragile beauty, softly built.

Branches creak, a haunting song,
Carried gently, flowing strong.
Tales of frost and chill that bite,
Nature's breath in purest white.

Stars above begin to twinkle,
Moonlight casts a silver sprinkle.
In the sway, a magic spun,
Where winter's warmth has just begun.

A tapestry of ice and wood,
Crystalline forests understood.
In the quiet, hearts take flight,
Swaying branches, pure delight.

Winter's Rustic Whimsy

Down the lane where snowflakes drift,
Winter whispers, soft and swift.
Rustic charms in frosty air,
Every breath, a jeweled flare.

Old barns dressed in coats of white,
Stand as guardians of the night.
Chimneys puffing dreams of fire,
Hearts are warmed by soft desire.

Icicles hang like glassy spears,
Echoing laughter, distant cheers.
Snowmen grin with coal-black eyes,
Childlike joy beneath the skies.

Wandering tales in the gloam,
Finding comfort, finding home.
Every flake a story spun,
Winter's whimsy has begun.

Beneath the stars, the world stands still,
A canvas bright, a heart to fill.
In rustic whispers, life unfolds,
Winter's charm, a tale retold.

Shards of Ice and Light

In the morning glow, they gleam,
Fragments caught in bright beams.
Each surface shines with fragile grace,
A dance of colors in winter's embrace.

Whispers of frost in the air,
Nature's artistry, rare and fair.
Crystals form a fleeting dream,
Shards of light, a silvery stream.

Underneath the freezing sky,
A tapestry where shadows lie.
Icicles hang like timeless art,
A cold elegance, a tender heart.

With every step, they crack and creak,
The world's beauty seems to speak.
In silence, the echoes reside,
Reflections of wonder, a frozen tide.

As daylight fades into the night,
Stars emerge, a twinkling sight.
Shards of ice, and the gathered light,
Weaves a magic, pure and bright.

The Embrace of the Stillness

In quiet moments, time stands still,
A gentle whisper, a heart to fill.
The world seems soft, wrapped in a sigh,
An invitation to breathe and lie.

Underneath the canopy wide,
Nature beckons, a place to hide.
In the stillness, dreams take flight,
Guided softly by the moon's light.

Trees sway gently with the breeze,
Whispers echo among the leaves.
Silent paths through shadowed glades,
A sanctuary where peace invades.

The stars above twinkle and gleam,
Cradling secrets, a cosmic dream.
In the embrace of night so tender,
The soul finds solace, sweet surrender.

Hold on to moments, brief yet bright,
In the stillness, find your light.
Embrace the silence, let it flow,
In the heart of stillness, love will grow.

Stains of Vibrance on a White Canvas

A splash of color, bold and free,
Brushstrokes dance with harmony.
On a canvas pure and wide,
Vibrance flows, a lively tide.

Crimson, azure, shades of gold,
Stories of the heart unfold.
A riot of hues in joyful sway,
Each stroke a memory, come what may.

Whispers of creativity sing,
In each corner, the colors spring.
Painting life with every hue,
Stains of passion, raw and true.

Splotches bold against the white,
A glimpse of dreams taking flight.
With every layer, magic grows,
A vibrant journey, nobody knows.

Bold expressions, gentle grace,
Artistry in every space.
Upon this canvas, time stands still,
Stains of vibrance, an endless thrill.

Dappled Lights in a Frozen World

Amidst the frost, a soft light shines,
Dapples dance on snow-white pines.
Sunbeams filtered through the trees,
Create a wonder, gentle breeze.

Each glimmer paints the world anew,
A fairytale in every view.
Underneath the icy veil,
Magic swirls in the cold tale.

Paths adorned with fleeting rays,
Nature's canvas in quiet displays.
In the stillness, shadows play,
Dappled lights brightening the day.

Glistening like a treasured dream,
Life reflected in a silver beam.
Frosted whispers, the winds applaud,
In a frozen world, beauty awed.

With every heartbeat, warmth ignites,
Through dappled lights, the spirit fights.
In winter's embrace, hearts will twirl,
Under the spell of a frozen world.

The Veil of Nature's Story

In whispers soft, the shadows play,
Beneath the boughs where night meets day.
Leaves curtail the moon's bright glance,
In nature's arms, we find romance.

The river hums a gentle tune,
Reflecting soft the silver moon.
While mountains wear their cloak of gray,
They hold the secrets of the day.

Each season paints its tale anew,
With blossoms bright and skies so blue.
In winter's breath, the stories freeze,
Yet in the spring, there's life to tease.

An echo of the past we trace,
In every leaf, a whispered face.
Nature weaves her woven art,
With threads of life, she plays the part.

From dawn till dusk, her stories flow,
In every breeze, a tale to know.
The veil of nature softly sways,
A tapestry of sunlight's rays.

Fireside Tales of Crimson and Ice

As shadows dance upon the wall,
The chair creaks low, the embers call.
With blankets wrapped, we gather near,
To weave the tales that draw us here.

The fire crackles, stories rise,
Of loves long lost and starry skies.
With whispers soft and laughter bright,
We chase away the winter's night.

Crimson flames like hearts aglow,
In every pause, the stories flow.
Of journeys ventured, dreams replete,
With every sip, our joys repeat.

Outside the frost paints windows white,
But here, our hearts feel warm and light.
In flickered light, we find our peace,
With words that make the cold decrease.

The tales entwine, like vines that twist,
In moments shared, we can't resist.
Fireside dreams in every sigh,
While winter whispers softly by.

A Dance of Fire and Frost

Beneath the skies where daylight blends,
A dance begins, where warmth descends.
The fire's glow, a passion bright,
While frost's embrace brings stillness tight.

In swirling mists, the colors chase,
As dawn unveils its gentle grace.
The flames flicker, the ice will gleam,
In nature's waltz, we find our dream.

They twirl beneath the watching stars,
A duet born of earth's memoirs.
Every spark a whisper told,
Of stories lost and ages old.

The crackling fire, a heartbeat strong,
While winter's song hums soft along.
Together bound, they spin and weave,
A tapestry we dare believe.

Embers dance with crystals bright,
Together brightening the night.
In this embrace, we find our place,
In harmony's warm, sweet grace.

Echoes of Color in the Cold

Through frosted panes, the colors gleam,
A palette rich, a vibrant dream.
The world outside in white dressed tight,
Hides whispered hues from our sight.

Yet in the heart, the colors bloom,
As warmth dispels the winter's gloom.
With every breath, the spirit sings,
Of hidden life that winter brings.

Sit quietly by the window's glow,
And watch the dance of winds that blow.
For even in the cold embrace,
The echoes of the warm days trace.

In red and gold, the visions bright,
Reflect the warmth of love's pure light.
While every flake that falls and drifts,
Is nature's way of giving gifts.

So hold the colors in your mind,
For in the cold, beauty's aligned.
With every chill that sweeps away,
The echoes of the warm will stay.

Crimson Berries in a Frozen Landscape

In the glisten of frost, berries glow bright,
Crimson jewels shining, a splendid sight.
Nature's delicate canvas, so cold and keen,
Amidst the stillness, a vibrant sheen.

Branches bow low, heavy with grace,
Each tiny berry, a warm embrace.
Winter whispers softly through the trees,
As life clings on, carried by the breeze.

Frozen petals dance in the crisp air,
While nature holds secrets she longs to share.
In the quiet, deep beauty begins,
A tale of resilience, where life never thins.

Lagging shadows stretch, as twilight lies,
Underneath twilight's soft, velvet skies.
Crimson bursts against the icy cloak,
A song of survival the still woods invoke.

In the heart of the chill, warmth finds a way,
As crimson berries brighten the gray.
With each tiny bead, hope's promise swells,
In a frozen landscape where wonder dwells.

Festive Green Amidst the Chill

Evergreen whispers in a frosty breath,
Festive adornments that dance with death.
Nature's embrace wears a sparkling shroud,
While shadows linger, soft and loud.

Sprigs of joy crown the winter's show,
With ribbons of gold, the cheer gathers flow.
Against the white, they defiantly stand,
A tale of persistence, beautifully planned.

Underneath stars that twinkle and shine,
The air is alive, with stories entwined.
Each branch tells a tale, rich and profound,
Of warmth in the cold, where solace is found.

As dusk descends, placing silver on green,
Festive glimmers paint a magical scene.
In the hush of the night, laughter resounds,
A melody carried on soft winter grounds.

In each moment of joy, life finds a way,
Embracing the chill of a wintry display.
Festive green sings to frosty winds' song,
Binding the seasons where hearts still belong.

Icy Blooms and Mirthful Memories

Icy blooms cradle the essence of time,
Whispers of laughter in frost's gentle climb.
In gardens of winter, they flourish and sway,
Holding the echoes of bright yesterday.

With petals like crystal, they shimmer and gleam,
Woven with memories, a spectral dream.
Each blossom a story, tenderly spun,
In the heart of the freeze, joy's web is run.

Sunlight's caress brings a fleeting embrace,
While shadows of night curtail their grace.
Yet in every glance, a flicker ignites,
Mirthful reflections in silvery lights.

As twilight deepens, the blooms nod with cheer,
Casting sweet laughter in the chill of the year.
A dance of the icy, a weave of delight,
Memories flourish as day turns to night.

In the stillness they thrive, bold and bright,
Icy blooms hold onto warmth's soft light.
Through the fingers of time, they gently embrace,
The spirit of moments, the warmth of each trace.

Nature's Garland of Gleam and Chill

Nature's garland sways in the winter breeze,
Gleams of frost adorning with elegant ease.
Every branch drapes soft whispers of white,
  Telling the magic of day turning night.

As the sun dips low, shadows gather and sway,
Amidst the still woods, where soft echoes play.
Glistening pathways through the snow they weave,
  Embracing the moment, inviting to leave.

In the hush of the dusk, peace blankets the land,
Each twinkle and shimmer, a delicate hand.
Nature holds court in her frosty domain,
Where silence and beauty intertwine like a chain.

Beneath the vast sky, stars begin to gleam,
  Crafting a tapestry, woven from dream.
Nature's garland glitters, each edge set in light,
  Embodying warmth in the heart of the night.

So pause for a moment, breathe deep and slow,
  Experience the magic that winter bestows.
In the embrace of the chill, find solace and grace,
  For nature's true beauty is time's warm embrace.

A Serenade of the Winter Woods

Whispers dance on frosty air,
Trees stand tall, a solemn prayer.
Snowflakes twirl in twilight's glow,
Nature's hush, a quiet show.

Footprints trace the winding trail,
Echoes of a winter's tale.
Moonlit shadows softly creep,
In the silence, secrets sleep.

Pine and fir, their scent so sweet,
Blankets white beneath our feet.
Winter's breath, a tender sigh,
In this haven, spirits fly.

Fireside warmth, a cherished night,
Stories shared in soft twilight.
From the woods, a song takes flight,
In the heart, pure delight.

Melodies in frozen air,
Nature sings, we stop and stare.
A serenade, the world so bright,
Winter's beauty, pure delight.

Unraveled Branches in the Chill

Barren limbs against the sky,
Whispers of the passing die.
Branches twist, entwined in frost,
Nature's wonders, never lost.

Crystals form on brittle bark,
Silent sentinels in the dark.
Each layer tells a winter's tale,
Echoes soft, like a ghostly veil.

In the stillness, time stands still,
Nature's breath, a gentle thrill.
Unraveled branches sway and bend,
Frozen whispers that we send.

The chill wraps round, a soft embrace,
Memories dance in a quiet space.
Nature's brush paints all in white,
A serene touch of pure delight.

Through the woods, a somber grace,
Every shadow finds its place.
In this beauty, we stand still,
Capturing the winter's chill.

Gems Adrift in Frozen Silence

Crystal droplets find their place,
Gems adrift in winter's grace.
Beneath the frost, a hidden glow,
Whispers of a world below.

Winter's breath, a soft embrace,
Nature's gems, we carefully trace.
Stars above in night's embrace,
Frozen silence, time and space.

In the stillness, beauty gleams,
Captured memories and dreams.
Each breath fogs the starry night,
In the dark, a glimmering light.

Nature's jewels, softly bright,
Reflecting every shade of white.
In the quiet, peace we find,
As gems adrift leave cares behind.

Stillness reigns, a sweet retreat,
In this winter's quiet beat.
For in the silence, treasures gleam,
Floating gently, like a dream.

The Color of Winter's Kiss

A palette draped in shades of gray,
Winter's kiss, the light of day.
Softest whispers, cool and bright,
Blushing pink at edge of night.

Frosted fields and skies so pale,
Color whispers on the gale.
Ivory blankets swirl and twirl,
As snowflakes dance, their edges curl.

The color of the icy breeze,
Eager branches bend with ease.
Winter's kiss upon the land,
A tender touch, a gentle hand.

Twilight weaves a silken thread,
In icy realms where dreams are bred.
Through the stillness, colors play,
Painting life in bright array.

Every hue, a story told,
In the winter's grasp, behold.
The color of each frozen sigh,
Winter's kiss, the world awry.

Winter's Embrace

The snowflakes fall, serene and light,
Blanketing the world in purest white.
Frosty whispers fill the air so still,
Nature sleeps wrapped in winter's will.

Branches glisten like diamonds in the sun,
Each breath of cold a tale that's begun.
Silent nights with stars that brightly gleam,
In winter's embrace, we find our dream.

Footprints mark a path through fields so wide,
Where laughter echoes, and spirits abide.
Gathering close, we share warmth and cheer,
In this chilly season, love draws near.

The fire crackles, a dance on the hearth,
Stories unfold, capturing our hearts.
With cups of cocoa, we savor the fire,
In winter's embrace, our souls inspire.

Under the stars, the world feels so small,
Yet within it glows a magic for all.
Embraced by the quiet, the still, the cold,
Winter whispers tales yet untold.

The Dance of Evergreen

The pines stand tall, in shades of deep green,
Whispering secrets, a sight so serene.
Beneath their boughs, the wild creatures play,
In the dance of evergreen, night meets day.

Winds weave through branches, a soft ballet,
Nature awakens, fresh scents on display.
Sunlight dapples the forest floor bright,
In the heart of the woods, all feels just right.

Chirping birds join the rhythmic refrain,
Celebrating life, joy mingles with rain.
Every drop glistens like jewels on the leaves,
In the dance of evergreen, the spirit believes.

Amidst the stillness, a harmony grows,
Life intertwined, as the river flows.
Each moment cherished, each heartbeat in tune,
In the dance of evergreen, under the moon.

Emerge from the shadows, embrace the light,
Step into nature, bask in her sight.
With every breath, let your worries dispel,
In the dance of evergreen, all is well.

Whispering Chill

The air turns crisp as twilight descends,
Whispers of chill on the breeze it sends.
Leaves rustle gently, a soft serenade,
In the heart of autumn, memories fade.

Fires flicker and glow, a warm embrace,
Sharing tales softly in this sacred space.
Wrapped in blankets, we gather near,
In the whispering chill, love is clear.

Moonlight dances on frost-kissed ground,
In the silence of night, peace is found.
Stars twinkle like diamonds across the skies,
In the whispering chill, wonder lies.

Each breath exhaled is a cloud in the air,
Painting the midnight with delicate care.
As laughter echoes, the world feels alive,
In the whispering chill, dreams thrive.

So come, let us wander where shadows play,
Embrace every moment, let worries sway.
In nature's embrace, find solace and will,
In the whispering chill, our hearts stay still.

Under the Icy Veil

Snowflakes twirl, a silent ballet,
Glistening softly under the icy veil.
Each breath of winter, crisp in the night,
Whispers enchant beneath moon's soft light.

Frosty patterns dance on windowpanes,
Nature's artistry, beauty remains.
Lost in the stillness, our spirits soar,
Under the icy veil, we seek to explore.

Branches bow low, weighed down with snow,
A world transformed, a magical show.
In this frozen wonder, time stands so still,
Under the icy veil, dreams gently thrill.

Footsteps muffled on a blanket of white,
Each moment savored, a delight in the night.
With hearts intertwined, we gather, we play,
Under the icy veil, love lights the way.

As dawn breaks softly, pink hues arise,
Nature awakens, a feast for our eyes.
In winter's embrace, let joy be our trail,
Forever enchanted under the icy veil.

Tales of Evergreen and Snow

In the forest deep and wide,
Evergreens stand with pride,
Shrouded in a cloak of white,
Whispers of the winter night.

Beneath their branches, silence weaves,
Stories caught in frosted leaves,
Echoes of the past abide,
In a world where dreams collide.

Snowflakes dance, a gentle race,
Kissing earth with soft embrace,
Time, a quiet, lingering friend,
In these woods where spirits blend.

Bright stars peek through twilight's veil,
Guiding those who seek the trail,
Of ancient tales that never fade,
In the heart of the glade.

So let us roam where shadows play,
In this wintry cabaret,
Each footstep marks a journey's flow,
In tales of evergreen and snow.

Revelry in the Frost

Underneath the silver sky,
Laughter rings as stars draw nigh,
Children play in frozen streams,
Chasing ever fleeting dreams.

Frosty branches, branches sway,
Mark the joy of winter's play,
Hot cocoa in gloved hands tight,
Hearts are warm on this cold night.

Candles flicker, shadows dance,
In the glow, we take a chance,
To make memories, bright and bold,
As stories of the season unfold.

Snowmen smile with carrot nose,
In this world where magic flows,
Twinkling lights adorn the trees,
A celebration in the breeze.

With every flake that graces earth,
We gather close, rejoice in mirth,
Such is the spirit, bright and true,
In revelry, we start anew.

The Bramble and the Shiver

In the thicket where shadows creep,
Secrets shared but never deep,
Bramble bushes, thorny guards,
With tangled roots and ancient shards.

A chilly breath upon the skin,
Awakens fears that dwell within,
Yet in the dark, a lantern glows,
Where courage blooms, and warmth bestows.

Mist wraps round with tender grace,
Veils the path that time won't trace,
A shiver runs, but hearts are bold,
In the mysteries of the cold.

Echoes of a haunting tune,
Drift like smoke beneath the moon,
Through the bramble, hope persists,
In the whispers of the mist.

So let us wander, hand in hand,
Through this wild and wintry land,
As the night sings low and clear,
In the bramble we find cheer.

Glimmering Shadows of Winter

Beneath the arch of frosted boughs,
Shadows dance, and time allows,
Glimmers caught in silver light,
Painting dreams of endless night.

Frozen rivers softly gleam,
Reflecting all that we can dream,
Each ripple tells a tale untold,
In the depths where whispers unfold.

Midnight skies in velvet spread,
Stars like jewels on winter's head,
In the quiet, beauty reigns,
Where the heart's hope gently gains.

Snow whispers secrets soft and light,
Carrying warmth on winter's bite,
By the fire, we weave our tales,
Of glimmering shadows and snowy trails.

So as the night encircles wide,
Let's find joy in winter's ride,
For in shadows, we find our way,
In glimmering dreams that play.

Milton Keynes UK
Ingram Content Group UK Ltd.
UKHW021359081224
452111UK00007B/105